# Wolf Point

Red Shuttleworth

STEPHEN F. AUSTIN STATE UNIVERSITY PRESS

Note:
The poems in this book, except for a handful of new pieces, are from
Bunchgrass Press chapbook anthologies published from 2012 to 2017.

ISBN: 978-1-62288-275-5

Production Manager: Kimberly Verhines
Author photo by Ciara Shuttleworth
Distributed by Texas A&M University Press Consortium

First Edition

*Sage-Steppe in Black & White*

# Wolf Point

# CONTENTS

ELLA
Why can't you cooperate?

EMMA
Because it's deadly. It leads to dying.

Sam Shepard
*Curse of the Starving Class*

## PROOF OF PURCHASE

The stink of a kangaroo rat
snagged and gnashed
by a Camry's busted AC
motor on a hot day.

# MAYBE ANOTHER TIME

Not every man does what is bidden.
Some cast stones.  Some take flight.

The cattlemen played poker,
traded identities, scattered cards on grass
half as tall as a bison's horns.

A thunderhead...
one of the devil's eyeballs.

Destitute wax figures in a museum.
Disarrangers in an old man's dream.

Ring of bells.  To walk the other way.

# MIRAGE AT GRAVEYARD-BORDER

Paper plates skitter down-street.
A crater-faced woman rinses her hands
at a water fountain… flint-eyes… crazed.

So much for the free, pre-rodeo, radio station
cheeseburger brunch near the post office.
The sweat-drenched banker and his
slice of peach pie, greasy napkins.

Soon the miracle of autumn.
Meteor nights.  Songs against darkness.
Bone particles upon high-desert wind.
Tattered door-to-door missionaries
from where a one-eyed man is king.

## IMPULSE AT IRREGULAR DECORUM

Praise the man who will not become a big decorative
wagon wheel on a tight-cropped tall-tales-of-money
lawn.

       Far better to have pitchfork... will travel.
There is darkness across *Home on the Range*.

See the glossy-black night street... humble rain upon
young Douglas Fir at odds with sidewalk planters
and no-core passersby.

         And I have run out of
contexts to yearn for.   Memory loss and wink.

# WINTER CHRONOGRAPH: 154

Icy dawn… yet tornados on the sun.
You're rolling daft from bed, hound whiskers
against your cheek. Pretty baby shifts deep
beneath a warm quilt. You're still in a dream…
juggling once-used on a red clay infield baseballs.

# THE WIND COMES

*Homage to Lermontov*

What is it to you, friend,
if a beggar eats cold ashes?

Days of black rain and slippery stone.
Nights of girls with flowers in their hair.

What if this, my friend, is where we
pitch tents for the night?

Lermontov: cavalry, women turning pale,
duels, transports of love, last time
secret meetings, kaleidoscopic vanity.

At age six, I wanted to be an angel
on a flame-red horse.  Brain-haze.
Sword-'n-pistol… midnight loopholes.

What is it to you,
if marble and dust are by chance?

# MULE-EAR, KNEE-HIGH BOOTS: FOUR POEMS

*Homage to Hagiwara*

A bite of love.
An icy-grim coyote pack.
Happiness-plums for sunrise.

~

*Ashes Canyon* after many funerals:
sluggish rattler and a gold clasp.
High pitched yips and barks.

~

Roses… dew-soaked boots.
Rain on a sun-faded farmyard sofa.
*Are you quite sure?*

~

The down-leg slide of a linen skirt
the color of a July wheat field.
Six ceramic coyotes trot single file.

## POCKET FULL OF QUARTERS

That tinny sound is coming from dark clouds.
The first sign of a crack-up.  Bourbon for the hound.

After his Miss Kansas wife left him, supper
at the basketball coach's house consisted of

hobo stew in boiled plastic bags.

It was much easier that year after I began parking
my emerald-green Ford Elite *behind* the saloon.

So it was that pretty baby and I stood
naked in a thunderstorm,
palms up, grinning for modest luck.

# NO MORE A CHILD

Early-up, old men set outside
a feed store, chew half-smoked cigars.
Gray darkness.  In the ramshackle
cafe across the dirt road, a waitress
aprons-up, puts on a semi-new Stetson,
looks outside at a battered '76 GMC pickup
as a rancher backs the truck onto a patch
of broken beer bottles.  Bacon grease
slow-warms in a couple of fry pans.

## WHEN THEY WASH THE DEAD

In this high-desert town, my first doctor
hailed from Khartoum.  Her family
owned slaves.  Everyone there
watched American westerns
and laughed… and laughed.

My second doctor, a grad
of Basrah University's med school,
enjoyed the fake hanging of himself
on CNN, for allegedly being
Saddam's beloved bastard son.
*No answers*, he said to me, *no answers*.

The coffin-crafter's children
place shiny-bright silver
dollars over the eyes of the dead.

## OLDEN DAYS

Any lovers' abyss
we are stone-thrown into.

Wall mice, stew
of gristle...
reindeer bones from Finland.

## SUMMER CHRONOGRAPH: 60

Late summer brown grass 'n weeds
'n rock.  Lots of loose volcanic rock.
You trudge cloudward without progress.
A huckleberry sunset to wish upon.
Freckled arthritic hands… joy of reata toss.

## SPRING CHRONOGRAPH: 39

Not one May angel, rebuked or beloved,
dangles in my sagebrush desert sky.
No jet plane.  A delphinium-azure silence.
A thousand rocky feet above sea level,
the Old West is all crumbled-out.

## FEBRUARY NOTE

Rain on ice. Snow. It's ponding
on the gravel two-track...
in our north pasture.

Lone coyote at the border of vision,
starvation-thin... injured back leg.

What you don't have, by right-now,
you sure as drizzlin' shit
ain't having.

# NEITHER LIGHT OF THE SUN

Battered sugar-white
pump house door
and a see-saw
midnight reflection:
dog and man on snow.

An ocean-sky of ebony scarves.

In the miles upon ether-exploded
sick room miles, we cursed
pain-worry.  Dog and man
on snow.  Winter-brown
thistle… north wind.
A bright angel approaches?

## MEDITATION ~ GNARLED SAGEBRUSH

*Death-of-nature* works best
in walnut-paneled rooms,
richly softened…
burgundy-velvet curtains,
lead-blue windows.

In the deeps of the moon.

# WHAT IS THE SPAN OF A CROW'S LIFE?

Cursed goathead thorn in the dog's muzzle.

Hard rain at Craters of the Moon.

Maybe illustrated Yeats theatre books.

Fields of autumn-blood stone.

Valentine's Day… pop of black-wing.

## LIKENESS

Freezing fog, ice puffs... faint snow.
Your rustic-yellow farmhouse...
bloodstains scrubbed-out
from four decades ago....

The Wolfhound puppy and you...
mosaic figures at-stumble
between fence-line juniper
and poplar: the frozen ground
is ghost ice... heaven-invisible.

## DESERT THISTLE…SUMMER'S END

Demon-thistle. Scream
of a burnt-red sunset cloud.
Truckloads of basalt pillars
for some town square decoration.

Oh, the error-prone dead.
Kiss the brow of a coyote skull…
for luck.

## ASSERTIONS AUTUMN

Local coyote reproduction
has fallen off. Mourning dove
feathers drift against sagebrush.

# SPRIG OF SAGEBRUSH

*You look good for a man of seventy-nine.*
Some cheery compliments
seal a man in resin.

~

Insomnia stripped to moonglow,
I chance to cut a sprig of sagebrush,
crush-rub it for the scent of sacred youth.

## STITCHES / WIRE

Jackson Pollock frequently
thought about off-black colors.
Approaches to lost youth…
Wyoming boots.

Beauty pageant girls
in tea-distressed linen.
We're speaking of creamy
smooth expanses.

Various stages of American self-erasure
include blood-painting with barb wire.

# JEROME, IDAHO

Bunched clouds were southbound…
for Nevada.  Summer hitchhikers,
thin rain ponchos, middle-fingered us.
A town too north to be named Geronimo.
At Dairy Queen, I ordered an Oreo Blizzard.
One side of her hair dyed blue,
the counter girl winked, spat the floor,
*This is the home of bottlecap hoarding.*

## PORTRAIT

To grow up knowing how
to hold your own death
like a library card…
and to place it
in a cupboard.
Perhaps field mice
would get it before
it got  you.  You imagined
you could learn on-the-run.

## PLEASE TELL US

Watch out for acquiring
a footprint on your tongue.

Fog always seemed
to come before heavy rain…
before the next lap dance.

Oh… saloon heartache.

Avoid those
frightened by desire.

Dust behind a jukebox.

Sharp dawn.

*This might require a measuring tape,*
one sheriff's deputy said to another.

## ROCK SPRINGS

Lesser schools and what you don't ask.
Glassy-eyed bison at a nearby ranch.
A UPS truck marbles past my motel.

Canned beans 'n franks heated
on a motel room hotplate.
Quart bottle of beer for a chaser.

The girl with the silver comb
is on a national tour to photograph
children's graves.  Turbulence.

Shouting demons.  TV screen blips.
Any flimsy excuse for a road trip.

## DISTANCE TO EMPTY: V

A hard December wind across sagebrush,
light rain… rough track to drive.  Broken rock.
No resemblance to swollen knuckles youth
swayed by bare breasts, Cadillac delusions…
Wild Turkey… Copenhagen nerve endings.

## FOUND RESTING

The rainy afternoon she sat
outside naked... hugging herself.

Abandoned sun-blistered
sage-steppe ranch.

A stack of laundered, creased
old corpse linen...
used over and over.

# IN THE GLOW BEFORE SLEEP

The kiss of a pale girl…
crippled since four.
Now. Turn and stillness.

Unseen blush.
Rain on the steeple outside.
Pale light from under the door.

Something in Trakl almost refuses.
No shame without absolute collapse.
*Who are you waiting for?*

*Our Lord.*

## READY TO SHOOT THE SCENE?

Stetsons, coffee mugs, fishing gear, hunting rifles, shirts and sweat-shirts, class rings, plaques, wedding licenses, passports, wedding photographs.... Truckloads go to thrift shops... to county dumps.

~

*Got to haul fat cattle to the kill plant in Toppenish. Pays rent. I'm a routine aspect of ghost country.*

## WOLF POINT

Rented a trashed, not yet cleaned motel room.
Derelict deer carcass on the asphalt parking lot.
Starved to death, someone chained the doe up,
drug it from the wind-socked side of town.

*How do I look?* She was in a blue ribbed sweater.

One kind of hollow can overlap with another kind.

It was three in the morning. She stroked my scars.

## BLIND-DRUNK FUMBLES

Your parents' only night... a San Francisco hotel named for
George Bernard Shaw. A heater-broke cold room. A hard nar-
row bed. Your mother, nineteen, professes distaste for Shaw,
prefers Joyce and the legends of Paris. Your father, twenty, from
the northwest corner of Tennessee, likes Shaw, because they have
the same first name. January 1944. A thrift bourbon bottle. She
takes off a simple homemade cotton dress... hands it to him. He
square-folds the dress, sets it on the seat of a wooden chair. Night
of repetition. A rain-streaked window... blink of the hotel sign
light. The after midnight rumble and steel grind of streetcars.
Awake. Nothing much to say.

# FRISCO PEAK

At six-thousand or so feet,
Beaver to the east…
Ely's Copper Queen to the west….

Clouds arrive to get lost.

On your back on the road…
little traffic… maybe you miss
her chestnut eyes.

Light patchouli wind.

## AUTUMNAL DAYBREAK

Ground fog off an irrigation canal…
Columbia River water.  Empty pages.
Maybe there's a sober past… a first wife.

*Graceland* has become an old song.
The Holy Ghost is wearing
James Joyce's Paris glasses.

I consider Eternity too often.
A silken bird circles over me…
wiggy with hunger, worn-out.

# BROWN GRASS

Great Plains museum drunken night.

House ~tarpaper shed~ north…
north of North Platte… and wind.

Town too small for a pawn shop.

*Stop your duplicitous lying.*
Schoolmarm says, *Terrifies me.*

Sometimes a warning's end-scream.

When the body was dug up,
it had turned black… mummified.

## SPOOL OF PICTURE-FRAME WIRE

Not quite alone, no.  Coyote yip-'n-bark.

# HOUR TO MIDNIGHT

A half-sister excommunicates me from family.
I'm like our father… barb wire.

A half-brother drops dead in his garden
at age 72.  It takes a year for news to reach.

A strong wind sweeps from Pinto Ridge.
Dry lightning.  Once… a note from Tom Russell,

*Jab Jab Jab, <u>Hook</u> the MOTHER FUCKERS.*
Unpacking Tyson Pro Standard Black Gloves.

# LONG PAST CEDAR CITY

Turned the talk to rawhide and hardwoods
in the now-closed small bar at the Ramada.
Two actresses in underwear were with me…
and a local poet (pieces on pigs) met us,
his teen daughter a tag-along.
The actresses smiled, laughed.

A life collaborating with coyotes.

Should I have bought the 19th century Lakota
coup stick in an antique store window?
One of the actresses, the redhead compensating
for something, gave me a pewter wine glass
from a dinner house…. Another
shop sold *Genuine Navajo* wolf pup
holy/ceremonial pipes. The other actress,
a blonde, looked like Bardot used to.

Railroad stations and hypnagogic voices.

## STONE-HEARTED SLEEP

You're in a restaurant,
busboy apron,
wiping water glasses
with a wet towel.

Or a museum of crash-dented cars.

Gregarious Angel of the Bottomless Pit.

Your bank robbery comrades Ned 'n Rupe,
bullet wounds and death-pale, all smiles.

Heart meds are turning knobs.

## PULLING INWARD

A crow sits a blackened telephone pole.
Somewhere a man with a fistful of camera
and a girl in an unzipped poster-red leather dress.

Last night you stared at a full moon.
You heard Jesus say to Peter,
*Come dine.* Two coyotes and a goat.

You used to wonder how long
your life would be.

RED SHUTTLEWORTH is the Western Heritage Wrangler
Award-winning author of *Woe to the Land Shadowing: Poems*. His
*Western Settings: Poems* received the first Western Writers of
America Spur Award. He was a 2017 Tanne Foundation Award-
recipient for playwriting and for poetry, which funded the
writing of *Americana West: A Century of Plays and Monologues*.

Printed in the USA
CPSIA information can be obtained
at www.ICGtesting.com
JSHW080603041224
74743JS00004B/18